Travel Guide To Sihanoukville 2024

Discover the Hidden Gems of Sihanoukville

Jason J. Jones

Table Of Content

INTRODUCTION

Sihanoukville: A Brief Overview

Travellers are drawn to Sihanoukville, which is tucked away on Cambodia's southwest coast and entices them with its immaculate beaches, lush tropical surroundings, and distinctive fusion of local and foreign cultures. Before we start our adventure through the Travel Guide to Sihanoukville in 2024, let's take a moment to briefly describe this amazing city.

1. Sihanoukville, also known as "Kampong Som" by the locals, is named after King Norodom Sihanouk, a significant person in local Cambodian history.

   Sihanoukville, which was founded as a port city in the late 1950s, was the main entry point for Cambodia from the coast. Its rise was facilitated by its advantageous location along the Gulf of Thailand, which also made it an important hub for trade.

2. The city's history is characterised by a fusion of elements, such as the architecture of French colonialism and the enduring Khmer spirit despite historical hardships.

   The city has experienced tremendous change in recent years, emerging as a bustling travel destination while preserving some of its historic charm.

3. The natural beauty of Sihanoukville is among its most alluring features. The city is endowed with several immaculate beaches, each with a distinct ambiance.

   Backpackers and party goers are drawn to Serendipity Beach because of its vibrant nightlife and hustle and bustle. Conversely, Otres Beach has a calmer, more relaxed atmosphere, making it ideal for anyone looking to unwind. Independence Beach, meanwhile, is a hidden treasure with serene shorelines and breathtaking sunsets.

4. Beyond its beaches, Sihanoukville has a variety of sights to see. A short drive away, Ream National Park is a nature lover's paradise.

   It is the perfect place for walking and bird viewing because it provides a verdant expanse of tropical woods, mangroves, and wildlife.

5. The local markets in Sihanoukville offer a glimpse into everyday life in Cambodia. These vibrant markets are filled to overflowing with vendors offering anything from handicrafts to

fresh seafood. Talking to local sellers can be a fun way to learn about their culture.

6. Sihanoukville is captivating due to its beautiful scenery and diverse cultural offers, but what makes it stand out are the undiscovered hidden jewels.

   The city's hidden gems include opportunities to fully immerse oneself in the native way of life, sacred temples steeped in history, and hidden waterfalls hidden away in lush jungles.

We shall examine Sihanoukville's nuances as we go deeper into this trip guide, giving you comprehensive insights into its activities, food options, attractions, and useful information.

In 2024, Sihanoukville will be more than just a place to visit; it will be an exciting journey with a wide range of activities to suit the interests of all types of tourists.

PLANNING YOUR TRIP

When to Visit

Your preferences for activities and weather will have a big impact on when is the best time to visit Sihanoukville. Below is a summary of the various seasons and when they are best for travel:

1. The busiest season to visit Sihanoukville is during the dry season, which runs from November to April. The temperature is fairly warm and the weather is dry.

    It's ideal for taking advantage of the stunning beaches and water activities. Since November through February are regarded as the busiest travel months, higher crowds and costs can be expected. If you would rather have a more laid-back trip, think about going in March or April.

2. May and June are considered the hot season. It can get very hot and muggy during this time, and there may be sporadic, light rain showers.

   Although it's less touristy than the dry season, some travellers may find the heat to be uncomfortable. Still, if you're ready for the weather, it can be a nice time to go.

3. July through October is considered the rainy season in Sihanoukville. During this time of year, there are often strong downpours and sporadic storms.

   During this period, a lot of outdoor activities and boat cruises might be cancelled. However, you can discover good lodging offers if you're searching for a less touristy, more affordable trip. Some tourists may find the area's abundant vegetation and the chance to take in its breathtaking natural surroundings intriguing.

In summary, the dry season, which runs from November to February, is the ideal time of year for most visitors to Sihanoukville.

The shoulder seasons, or even the rainy season, can present special chances to see the area if you'd rather have a less expensive and congested experience. Verify the exact weather predictions for the dates of your trip and make plans appropriately.

Visa and Entry Requirements

Understanding Cambodia's visa and entry regulations is crucial while organising a vacation to Sihanoukville. Here's a summary of the essential information:

Visa prerequisites:

Tourist Visa: To enter Cambodia, most visitors need a tourist visa. One of the following methods is available for obtaining a tourist visa:

1. **Visa on Arrival (VOA):** At Phnom Penh International Airport, Siem Reap International Airport, and certain land border crossings, travellers from a variety of nations can receive a visa upon arrival.

   The 30-day validity period of this visa can typically be extended for an extra 30-day period.

2. **E-Visa:** Before your journey, you can apply online for an e-visa. It's a practical choice that enables quicker processing at the border crossing. Additionally, the 30-day validity of the e-visa can be extended.

3. **Cambodian Embassy or Consulate**: In your home country, you can apply ahead of time for a tourist visa to a Cambodian embassy or consulate.

4. **Business Visa:** You'll need a business visa, which usually needs sponsorship from a Cambodian firm or group if you intend to operate or conduct business in Cambodia.

5. **Long-Term Visa**: There are special visa options available if you plan to stay in Cambodia for a lengthy period, such as for volunteer work or retirement.

These include volunteer and retirement visas.

Entry prerequisites:

When travelling to Cambodia, be ready for the following:

1. **Passport**: Verify that the validity of your passport extends at least six months after the date you plan to leave Cambodia.

2. **Visa charge:** Have US money ready to cover the visa charge. Depending on the type of visa and your country of origin, the fee could change.

3. **Passport Photo:** You might need to provide a current passport-sized photo when applying for a visa.

4. **Immigration Form**: When you arrive, you will need to fill out an immigration form. You will need the departure section of this form when you depart the country, so keep it safe.

5. **Visa Extensions**: You can normally contact the immigration office in Sihanoukville or other neighbouring locations if you want to remain longer than the allowed time on your visa.

   To avoid any overstay fines, it is best to begin the extension process before the expiration of your visa.

Before your journey, always confirm the most recent visa and entrance requirements on the official website of the Royal Embassy of Cambodia or the embassy or consulate of your nation in Cambodia. Fulfilling these prerequisites is essential to guarantee a seamless arrival and stay in Sihanoukville, Cambodia.

Accommodation Options

Sihanoukville provides a variety of lodging choices to accommodate different tastes and price ranges. You can locate lodging that suits your needs, whether you're looking for opulent seaside resorts, affordable guesthouses, or somewhere in between. The following are a few popular places to stay in Sihanoukville:

1. **Beachfront Resorts**: There are several opulent beachfront resorts in Sihanoukville, offering first-rate amenities, stunning scenery, and easy access to the beach.

   These resorts frequently have restaurants, bars, spas, and swimming pools. They provide tourists seeking an upscale encounter.

2. **Boutique Hotels**: A more personal and distinctive atmosphere can be found at boutique hotels. They are available in a range of sizes and types, frequently with unique charm, chic décor, and personalised services.

3. **Mid-Range Hotels**: Sihanoukville is home to several mid-range hotels that provide cosy lodgings with features like Wi-Fi, air conditioning, and on-site eating options. Travellers seeking a hotel that strikes a balance between comfort and price may consider these options.

4. Hostels and guesthouses abound in Sihanoukville, particularly in the Serendipity Beach neighbourhood. These are inexpensive choices with

limited amenities that are perfect for tourists on a tight budget or backpackers. They frequently have private rooms or beds in dorms.

5. **Holiday Rentals**: Some travellers have a preference for short- or long-term holiday rentals, such as villas, flats, or bungalows.

   This choice offers a cosier atmosphere and can have kitchen amenities.

6. **Eco-Friendly Lodges:** There are lodges and bungalows tucked away in the outdoors for tourists looking for environmentally conscious and sustainable lodging.

   These resorts frequently place a high value on eco-friendly activities and ecotourism excursions.

7. **Hostels**: Hostels are an excellent option if you're travelling alone or want to meet other travellers. Backpacker hostels in Sihanoukville are well-known for their planned events, inexpensive rates, and friendly atmosphere.

8. **Camping and Glamping**: You can immerse yourself in nature and have a more adventurous stay in some of the surrounding locations of Sihanoukville by going camping or glamping (glamorous camping).

9. **Long-Term Rentals**: Long-term rentals are an option for those who intend to stay in Sihanoukville for a longer period. For a monthly or annual lease, you can locate houses or apartments.

It's a good idea to reserve your lodging in advance, particularly from November to February when travel is at its busiest. The sort of hotel you choose in Sihanoukville will mostly depend on your tastes, financial situation, and desired kind of experience. This coastal paradise offers accommodations that meet your needs, whether you're searching for adventure, relaxation, or a combination of the two.

Packing Essentials

You must pack for your vacation to Sihanoukville, Cambodia, to guarantee a relaxing and pleasurable stay. Here is a list of necessities that you should think about putting in your packing list:

Travel Records:

- Visa and passport (if needed).
- copies of significant papers that are kept apart from the originals in storage.

- Specifics of travel insurance.

Clothes:

- Wear clothing that is breathable and lightweight for the tropical weather.
- swimwear for the stunning beaches.
- sun-protective apparel, such as sunglasses and hats.
- Flip-flops, sandals, and comfy walking shoes.
- During the rainy season, pack a lightweight rain jacket or poncho for those infrequent downpours.

toiletries

- High SPF sunscreen.
- repellent for insects.
- Toiletries such as toothbrush, shampoo, conditioner, and soap (you should bring your own, though some accommodations may supply these).

- Any prescribed drugs as well as a basic first aid package.
- Hand sanitizer and toilet paper in travel sizes.

Technology:

- Power converters and adapters (Type A, C, and G sockets are used in Cambodia).
- cellphone and its charger.
- a smartphone or camera to record memories.
- When travelling, use a power bank to keep your electronics charged.

Cash and Safety:

- Local cash for minor purchases and emergencies, such as US dollars or Cambodian Riel.
- To keep your valuables safe, use a money belt or travel wallet.

- Padlock to keep your belongings safe or your dorm locker locked.
- a copy of your policy for travel insurance.

Unspecified:

- To stay hydrated, use reusable water bottles instead of single-use plastic ones.
- Atlas or travel guide for Sihanoukville.
- snorkelling equipment if you want to see the stunning underwater scenery.
- Sarong or beach towel.
- any particular equipment or supplies required for outdoor pursuits like diving, water sports, or hiking.
- To separate damp or filthy clothes, use plastic bags.

For amusement:
- For leisure time, use books, an e-reader, or entertainment gadgets.

- interacting socially with other tourists through card games or travel games.

Local Number to Contact:

- Jot down the address and phone number of your lodging, as well as the contact details for any friends or local guides you intend to meet.

Always prioritise goods you'll need and pack light. Sihanoukville's laid-back vibe makes it simple to dress casually, and if needed, you can buy a lot of things locally.

When travelling, consider the impact on the environment and use reusable bags and eco-friendly products to lessen your impact. Finally, remember to adjust your packing list based on the weather forecast for the dates of your trip.

GETTING TO SIHANOUKVILLE

Transportation Options

To assist you in moving around the city and taking in the surrounding sights, Sihanoukville has a range of transportation choices. The following are a few popular modes of transportation that are available to tourists:

1. Tuk-tuks are a well-liked and reasonably priced mode of transportation for short trips inside Sihanoukville.

   These motorised rickshaws are excellent for short travels within the city or to neighbouring beaches because they can hold multiple passengers. Before the ride, haggle over the fare.

2. **Motorbike Taxis:** Known as "motodops" in the area, motorbike taxis are easily accessible and can get you to your destination more quickly than tuk-tuks, particularly in congested areas. A helmet should be worn, and the fare should be negotiated beforehand.

3. **Rental Motorbikes and Scooters:** Independent tourists frequently choose to rent a motorbike or scooter. It offers freedom and the chance to go at your speed when exploring.

   You'll need a Cambodian licence or an international driver's licence. Don't forget to wear a helmet and abide by traffic laws in the area.

4. **Bicycles**: Riding a bike is a green way to go around Sihanoukville and its environs. Bicycle rentals are available

from many lodging options, and they're a terrific way to see the city's more sedate areas and beautiful locations.

5. **Local Buses**: If you're looking for an affordable method to go around Sihanoukville, the city provides a local bus system. These shared minivan buses are referred to as "samlors".

6. **Private Car Rental**: If you're travelling in a group or have a lot of luggage, renting a private car or minivan with a driver can be more comfortable and convenient. This is a good choice for short excursions or local exploration.

7. **Boats and Ferries**: From Sihanoukville's harbour, you can take a boat or ferry to neighbouring islands including Koh Rong and Koh Rong Samloem. It is imperative to confirm in advance as

there are several ferry services available and schedules that differ.

8. **Taxis**: Compared to larger cities like Phnom Penh, metered taxis are less popular in Sihanoukville. Nonetheless, taxi services are available, and certain lodging options may set them up for you.

9. **App-Based Ride Services**: Sihanoukville is home to a few ride-sharing applications, including PassApp and Grab.

   These apps frequently offer upfront pricing and might be useful for hailing transportation.

10. **Walking**: Sihanoukville is a fantastic way to discover local markets, restaurants, and other attractions

because of its compact city centre and pedestrian-friendly coastal regions.

Remember that there might not be as much developed road infrastructure as in certain other locations and that traffic conditions can change.

When utilising motorbike taxis, rental scooters, or bicycles, put safety first, wear a helmet, and obey traffic laws in your area. When using non-metered transportation choices, always settle on fares in advance to prevent confusion.

Arrival at Sihanouk International Airport

Your trip to discover Sihanoukville and its stunning surroundings begins when you land at Sihanouk International Airport. Here's what to anticipate when you get to the airport:

1. **Immigration and Customs:**

- Once you step off the aircraft, you'll head to the immigration section.
- Your passport, any necessary visas, and the completed immigration forms must be presented.
- Your admission into Cambodia will be processed by immigration officers. There may be lines, so exercise patience, especially during busy travel periods.

2. **Arrival Visa (VOA):**

- You can apply for a tourist visa on arrival if you haven't already gotten one in advance. In the immigration area are counters for applying for visas.

- Complete the application for a visa and attach a passport-sized photo.
- The visa fee must be paid in US dollars, cash only.
- You'll get a visa sticker on your passport once your application has been finalised.

3. **Claim for Baggage:**

- Once you have cleared immigration, go to the baggage claim area to pick up your checked bags. Make sure your luggage claim tags are prepared for examination.

4. **Clearance from Customs:**

- Once your bags are collected, you will have to proceed through customs processing. This usually entails a quick check of your luggage or a customs statement.

5. **Services at Airports:**

- Despite its modest size, Sihanouk International Airport has all of the standard amenities, such as currency exchange, ATMs, and vehicle rental desks.

6. **Modes of Transportation:**

- There are several ways to get from the airport terminal to your Sihanoukville lodging when you leave. Taxis, shuttle services, and uk-tuks are widely accessible. Along with your lodging, you can also schedule your transportation in advance.

7. **Regional Data:**

- There's normally a tourist information desk or a desk for information about local services and attractions if you need help or have any inquiries.

8. **Linguistic:**

- Although English is commonly understood, especially in tourist regions, Khmer is the official language. Speaking English with airport and transportation staff should be easy for you.

9. **Crucial Reminders**

- Cash in US dollars is recommended for initial expenses and visa fees.

- Safeguard your visa, passport, and other vital papers.

- Watch out for possible fraud or overcharging by unregistered tuk-tuk or taxi drivers. Before your trip, it's a good idea to agree on fares.

The process of arriving at Sihanouk International Airport is not too complicated. After passing through immigration and customs, you'll be all set to start exploring Sihanoukville and the breathtaking Cambodian coastal regions.

Travelling by Land or Sea

Sihanoukville is a coastal town that can be reached through a variety of transportation methods, making land or sea travel a thrilling journey. The two main routes to Sihanoukville are as follows:

1. Getting Around by Land:

- Bus: Travelling by bus is one of the most popular ways to get to

Sihanoukville. From Phnom Penh or other major Cambodian cities, buses are an option. There are several bus kinds available, from basic to more opulent models with air conditioning.

It usually takes four to six hours to get there from Phnom Penh, depending on traffic and road conditions.

- **Private Transfer**: You can schedule a private automobile or minivan with a driver if you'd like a more relaxing and private trip.

For individuals who like to travel independently or in larger groups, this is a great alternative. It permits stops along the route to take in the many views and attractions.

- Shared Minivans: Another choice for land travel is the shared minivan service. Although these minivans can be more crowded than buses, they are a quicker method to get to Sihanoukville.

2. **Taking a Sea Trip:**

- Ferries and Speedboats: Koh Rong and Koh Rong Samloem, two neighbouring islands, are accessible from Sihanoukville. From the Sihanoukville port, speed boats and ferries run, offering easy access to these idyllic island getaways.

  In addition to being a mode of transportation, travelling by boat offers breathtaking views of the coastline.

- **Day tours:** If you're looking for a fun way to explore the area, a few tour companies in Sihanoukville offer day tours by boat to neighbouring islands.

The following elements should be taken into account while choosing between flying or sailing to Sihanoukville:

1. **Time and Convenience:** Land transportation can be more flexible about stops and detours along the route, and it may also be more time-efficient.

   If your destination is one of the neighbouring islands, travelling by boat is the best option since it provides a direct and picturesque path.

2. **Comfort and Cost:** There are several options for land travel, ranging from inexpensive private transfers to basic buses, depending on your preferences. Ferry or speedboat services are typically used for sea transit to the

islands; these services can differ in terms of cost and comfort.

3. **Destination**: The decision you make may also be influenced by where you end up going. Getting to Sihanoukville itself is best done by ground transportation. You will need to travel by water if you intend to explore the islands.

4. **Adventure & Experience:** Land travel lets you see the surrounding landscape and local way of life, while sea travel offers a distinctive coastal experience.

Regardless of the mode of transportation you select, land and water alternatives each have their benefits and allure, giving visitors a variety of ways to experience Sihanoukville and its environs' coastal splendour.

TOP ATTRACTIONS

Serendipity Beach

Among the busiest and most lively beaches in Sihanoukville, Cambodia, is Serendipity Beach. It's well known for a variety of water sports and activities, beachside bars, and a vibrant atmosphere. What to anticipate when visiting Serendipity Beach is as follows:

1. Beach Feelings

- The vibrant and convivial ambiance of Serendipity Beach is well-known. A mixture of residents, tourists, and backpackers may be seen taking advantage of the sea, sand, and sun.

2. Restaurants and Bars on the Beach:

- Numerous eateries and pubs serve a range of dishes and alcohol along the shore. There are many places to sit along the beach, offering great views of the water.

3. Activities in Water:

- The best place to go for water sports and activities is Serendipity Beach. Paddleboarding, jet skiing, parasailing, and even boat trips to other islands are available.

4. Purchasing and Keepsakes:

- There are stands and tiny stores along the beach road that sell jewellery, clothes, souvenirs, and handcrafted goods from the area.

5. After Dark:

- Beach parties, live music, and a vibrant nightlife scene make the beach come alive at night. It's a well-liked location for people who like to mingle and dance when the sun goes down.

6. **Modifications**:

- There are several different types of lodging at Serendipity Beach, ranging from mid-range hotels to inexpensive hostels. Many of these locations have easy access to the sea and views of the beach.

7. **Convenient Attractions**

- The central market and Ochheuteal Beach are two other Sihanoukville attractions that are near Serendipity Beach. It's also a handy place to begin your exploration of Ream National Park.

8. **Views of the Sunset and Relaxation:**

- Even while Serendipity Beach has a vibrant atmosphere, there are also calmer areas where you can unwind and take in breathtaking views of the Gulf of Thailand at sunset.

It is noteworthy that Serendipity Beach is a frequently visited site that can get congested, particularly during the busiest travel season. The neighbouring Otres Beach would be a better choice if you'd rather have a more sedate beach experience.

But Serendipity Beach is a great choice if you're looking for a lively, social environment with lots of entertainment alternatives. For tourists wishing to take in the most of Sihanoukville's beach scene, it serves as a major hub.

Otres Beach

In Sihanoukville, Cambodia, Otres Beach offers a calmer, more subdued vibe than Serendipity Beach. What to anticipate when visiting Otres Beach is as follows:

1. Calm Environment:

- Otres Beach is renowned for its tranquil and relaxed atmosphere. It's a location to relax, take in the scenery, and get away from the bustle of the city.

2. Gorgeous Beach:

- The beach itself has lovely seas and soft white sand. It is well-maintained. It's the perfect place to swim and relax.

3. Modifications:

- A variety of lodging options are available at Otres Beach, ranging from eco-friendly bungalows and mid-range resorts to affordable guesthouses. There are beachfront locations with breathtaking views of the ocean and convenient access to the water.

4. **Eating**

- Numerous eateries and pubs serve a range of regional and foreign cuisines along the shore.

  While sipping on fresh seafood, vegetarian selections, and mixed drinks, you may take in the sound of the breaking waves.

5. **Activities and Sports on the Water:**

- Even while Otres Beach is more of a place to unwind, there are still things to do like paddleboarding, kayaking, and boat cruises to other islands. It's a fantastic location for casual water exploration.

6. **Well-being and Yoga:**

- A lot of lodging options provide yoga courses and wellness retreats, which makes Otres Beach a well-liked option for travellers looking for spiritual health and relaxation.

7. **Dusks**:

- Otres Beach is well-known for its magnificent dusks. Choose a comfortable position on the beach as the day comes to an end to watch the sunset.

8. **Availability**:

- Otres Beach can be reached from Sihanoukville's city centre in about 20 minutes by motorbike or tuk-tuk. It's a handy way to get away from the city without sacrificing accessibility.

9. Local Culture and Community:

- Otres Beach and the surrounding area have a distinct and inviting feel because of the close-knit community of natives and expats. Interact with the amiable residents who make this location their home.

10. Eco-Friendly Travel:

- Otres Beach is renowned for its dedication to environmentally responsible and sustainable activities.

  A lot of local establishments, including lodging facilities, prioritise reducing their environmental footprint.

Otres Beach is a great option in Sihanoukville if you're looking for a quieter, more private beach experience.

It's a spot to unwind, get in touch with nature, and savour the small joys of beach living—all while being near enough to the city to allow you to visit other sites whenever it's convenient for you.

Independence Beach

Independence Beach in Sihanoukville, Cambodia is a lovely, less busy beach that is also referred to as Independence 4 Beach or Hawaii Beach. When visiting Independence Beach, you should anticipate the following:

1. Peaceful Environment:

- Independence Beach is renowned for its calm and peaceful environment. It's a tranquil diversion from Sihanoukville's more crowded beaches.

2. The Pristine Coast:

- The beach has lovely, turquoise waves and soft, golden sands. It's a great place for lounging, swimming, and tanning.

3. Modifications:

- While there aren't as many lodging options right on Independence Beach as there are on other Sihanoukville beaches.

  There are a few beachside resorts and guesthouses that provide tranquil surroundings with views of the sea.

4. Meal Selections:

- A variety of regional and global dishes are available at a few eateries and seaside bars. It's a terrific spot to eat different cuisines and fresh seafood while taking in the sound of the waves.

5. Water Activities:

- Even though Independence Beach is more sedate, you can still engage in watersports like paddleboarding and kayaking. Local providers offer equipment for rent.

6. Scenic Outlooks:

- It's well known that the beach has amazing sunsets. Watch the sunset over the placid waters of the Gulf of Thailand as the day draws to a close.

7. Convenient Attractions

- The Independence Monument and the neighbouring Sokha Beach Resort, which has a casino and spa amenities, are two of the attractions that are adjacent to Independence Beach.

8. Historische Bedeutung:

- The beach has the name of the day on November 9, 1953, when Cambodia declared its independence from France. A reminder of this momentous occasion is the neighbouring Independence Monument.

9. Availability:

- Independence Beach is ideally situated inside Sihanoukville, making it simple to get to from the city centre on a motorbike or tuk-tuk.

10. **Calm Withdrawal**:

- For those who want a more sedate and peaceful beach experience, Independence Beach is a great option.

  For those who wish to unwind and take in the breathtaking scenery of Cambodia's coastline, it's ideal.

Independence Beach is a fantastic choice if you're searching for a quiet, less crowded beach location where you can take in a more carefree and laid-back ambiance. It offers a peaceful haven with easy access to all of Sihanoukville's facilities and activities.

Ream National Park

A stunning natural wonder close to Sihanoukville in Cambodia is called Ream National Park. Travellers wishing to experience tropical scenery, tranquil streams, and abundant biodiversity will find it to be a unique and protected habitat. What to anticipate when visiting Ream National Park is as follows:

1. innate beauty

- Ream National Park is renowned for its breathtaking natural scenery, which includes rivers, mangroves, lush tropical rainforests, and immaculate beaches. It's a great place for outdoor adventurers and nature lovers to visit.

2. Observing Wildlife:

- Numerous bird species, primates, reptiles, and aquatic life are among the vast array of animals that can be found in the park. Seeing uncommon and exotic animals in their native habitat is possible when participating in the popular hobby of birdwatching.

3. **Hiking & Trekking:**

- Numerous hiking and trekking paths in Ream National Park take you through verdant jungles and to picturesque vantage spots.

  With the help of knowledgeable local guides who can impart their knowledge of the local flora and animals, you can explore the park on foot.

4. **Boat Journeys:**

- A well-liked method of seeing the park's rivers is through boat cruises. You can tour estuaries and mangrove forests, go kayaking, or take a riverboat cruise. These excursions provide you with the chance to observe the traditional fishing methods and local fishing villages.

5. **Wildlife Refuge:**

- A section of the park functions as a wildlife sanctuary, aiding in the preservation and rehabilitation of threatened species like pileated gibbons and fishing cats.

6. **Spotless Beaches:**

- Ream National Park is home to several stunning, lesser-known beaches including Koh Sampouch Beach, which provide a peaceful setting for unwinding and tanning.

7. **Outings:**

- For those who like to be closer to nature, camping is permitted in several areas of the park, offering an immersive and genuine experience. Be ready for a rustic adventure because camping amenities are rudimentary.

8. **Opportunities for Education and Ecotourism:**

- The park wants to encourage tourists and conservation. You may discover the significance of preserving Cambodia's natural resources as well as the park's conservation initiatives.

9. **Enjoying a picnic and appreciating nature:**

- Many guests love having picnics in the park's picturesque spots where they can take in the tranquil atmosphere and the sounds of nature.

10. **Convenience**:

- From Sihanoukville, Ream National Park is reachable by automobile, motorcycle, or tuk-tuk. The ride from the city centre to the park's entrance is brief and enjoyable.

11. **Conscientious Travel:**

- It's critical to engage in responsible tourism by observing park regulations and protecting the ecosystem. Refrain from disturbing or feeding wildlife, as well as from littering.

Ream National Park presents an amazing chance to see the natural splendour of Cambodia, discover its varied ecosystems, and establish a bond with its fauna. For those who appreciate the outdoors and adventure in the Sihanoukville area, this park is a must-visit, whether their interests lie in trekking, birdwatching, or just relaxing outside time.

HIDDEN GEMS

Secret Waterfalls

The hidden waterfalls in Sihanoukville and the surrounding environs are well-known for providing a distinctive, off-the-beaten-path experience. Adventurers who desire to discover Cambodia's natural beauty will love these remote waterfalls. Here are a few hidden waterfalls to find:

1. Waterfall Kbal Chhay:

- The distance between Kbal Chhay Waterfall and Sihanoukville is roughly 16 kilometres.

  It's not quite a "secret" waterfall, but it is more peaceful and calmer than some of the more well-known nearby attractions because fewer people visit it.

- This waterfall offers places to swim, have a picnic, and unwind. It is surrounded by beautiful vegetation and boasts a succession of waterfalls. It's a great location to get away from the throng and take in the peace of nature.

2. Waterfall Chhay Areng:

- Slightly farther out from Sihanoukville, the more secluded and lesser-known Chhay Areng Waterfall is a hidden treasure.

  It is located close to the Cardamom Mountains in the southwest of Cambodia, in the Areng Valley.

- Travelling to the Chhay Areng Waterfall requires passing through isolated communities and rocky terrain. The waterfall is a stunning, multi-tiered cascade that empties into a cool pool.

In this immaculate natural location, swimming and the tranquil mood are enjoyable.

3. **Popokvil Falls:**

- It takes a little while to get to Popokvil Waterfall in Bokor National Park from Sihanoukville. It's not hidden, but compared to other park attractions, it's not as popular.

- The trail leading to the waterfall, which is tucked away in the jungle, is both picturesque and thrilling. A cool swim is ideal in the pool at the base of the waterfall. Moreover, there is a wealth of vegetation and fauna in the nearby forest.

Experience a more serene and secluded setting while fostering a connection with the natural world at these hidden waterfalls.

While some of these waterfalls are not identified, local expertise can be crucial for a safe and enjoyable visit. If you want to explore these hidden gems, think about hiring a guide.

It may take some work to get to these hidden waterfalls, but the peace and natural beauty make the trip worthwhile. You should also be ready for some off-road driving and trekking.

Local Markets

Discovering Sihanoukville's local markets can be a great way to experience Cambodian culture firsthand, try the local food, and browse souvenir shops. You can attend the following local markets in Sihanoukville:

1. The largest and most well-known market in Sihanoukville is called Phsar Leu Market. This place has a huge

selection of goods, such as jewellery, gadgets, fresh produce, seafood, apparel, and souvenirs. The market is a thriving and busy place to explore the way of life in the area.

2. **Phsar Leu Tech Market:** This smaller, more specialised market, which is close to Phsar Leu Market, specialises mostly in fresh seafood.

In addition to seeing fishermen unload their daily haul, a variety of seafood is available for purchase. It's an excellent spot to eat seafood meals at the local restaurants.

3. **Phsar Do Dum Market:** Known for its seafood, this market is located close to Victory Beach. At the market's restaurants, you may purchase fresh fish and have it prepared, making for a distinctive dining experience.

4. **Otres Market:** Situated in Otres Village, Otres Market has an atmosphere distinct from that of typical Cambodian markets. With a concentration on locally created art, jewellery, clothes, and crafts, it's more of an artsy and bohemian market. It's a terrific location to get unusual presents and mementos.

5. **Sihanoukville Night Market:** This market is set up on the seaside in Sihanoukville during the evening, mostly on weekends.

   There are numerous street food vendors, crafts sellers, and live entertainment options. It's a great place to savour regional cuisine and take in the ambiance of the beach.

6. **Street Markets**: In addition to these particular markets, Sihanoukville is

home to a plethora of tiny markets and street sellers. These sellers frequently offer a selection of regional candies, fruits, and daily necessities.

Since haggling is widespread in Cambodian markets, don't forget to practise your negotiating abilities while touring these markets. Be ready to sample some delectable snacks and street food from Cambodia as well.

Local markets are an integral part of your Sihanoukville experience since they provide an authentic window into the everyday routine and culture of the area, making them more than just places to purchase.

Cultural Experiences

Sihanoukville is renowned for its stunning beaches and surrounding natural features, but the area also offers rich cultural activities. Embrace the local way of life in the following ways:

1. **Explore Local Temples**: Pay a visit to Wat Leu and Wat Krom, two Buddhist temples. Engage with the monks and see the rites. Keep in mind to show respect and wear modest clothing when you visit places of worship.

2. Take a Cooking Class to learn how to prepare authentic Cambodian food. To gain an understanding of Cambodian cuisine, cooking sessions frequently involve a trip to the neighbourhood market to buy goods.

3. Watch Traditional Khmer Dance Performances: Experience the rich

cultural legacy of Cambodia through traditional Khmer dance performances. These performances are available at many Sihanoukville restaurants and hotels.

4. **Local Festivals & Events**: For information on cultural festivals and events, consult the local event calendar. Among the main festivities with cultural significance are Pchum Ben (Ancestor's Day), the Water Festival (Bon Om Touk), and the Cambodian New Year.

5. Learn as much as you can about the Khmer language, including the alphabet and a few simple words. When tourists attempt to speak with them in their language, the locals are appreciative.

6. **Visit Neighbouring Towns**: Get to know the locals by travelling to other towns. Volunteering or participating in homestays can offer profound cultural insights.

7. Attend workshops on traditional handicrafts made by the Khmer people, such as basketry, pottery, and silk weaving.

   These activities provide you the opportunity to make your mementos in addition to showcasing the workmanship of the area.

8. **Investigate Local Markets:** Go around, talk to vendors, and try some street cuisine. It's a fantastic way to get a taste of Cambodian daily life.

9. Visit the Sihanoukville Autonomous Port and the Ream National Park

Environmental Education Center to learn about Cambodian history. Both locations provide educational opportunities regarding the history and maritime activity of the area.

10. **Ecotourism and Sustainable Tourism:** Take part in ecotourism endeavours that support community development and environmental preservation.

Sustainable tourism practices are the emphasis of certain local tour providers.

11. **Opportunities for Volunteering:** If you'd like to give back, think about volunteering with charities and local organisations that focus on education and community development.

Though they may not be as prevalent as in other regions of Cambodia, cultural activities in Sihanoukville provide insight into the customs and daily lives of the local Khmer populace. You can learn more about the area and its inhabitants by getting involved in cultural events and interacting with the local population.

WHERE TO EAT AND DRINK

Local Cuisine

The cuisine of Cambodia is a delicious fusion of flavours, derived from French and Southeast Asian cooking customs. You may enjoy a wide range of mouthwatering regional cuisine while in Sihanoukville. Some of the best Cambodian foods and delicacies to sample are as follows:

1. **Amok**: The national dish of Cambodia is a must-try, amok. It's a fragrant curry cooked with coconut milk and banana leaves that's usually served with fish, poultry, or tofu. Its distinct flavour comes from the fusion of galangal, kaffir lime, and lemongrass.

2. Bai Sach Chrouk is a well-liked morning meal in Cambodia. It is made up of rice, pickled veggies on the side,

and grilled pork that is frequently served with a fried egg.

3. **Kuy Teav:** Available in a variety of flavours, Kuy Teav is a tasty noodle soup. Rice noodles, a flavorful broth, and your selection of meat or seafood are usually included. To alter the flavour, add chile, lime, and herbs.

4. **Lok Lak:** A stir-fried dish made with marinated chicken or beef, accompanied by a black Kampot pepper and lime dipping sauce. It's typically served with tomatoes and lettuce.

5. **Prahok**: A staple of Cambodian cooking, prahok is a fermented fish paste. It is used in many different recipes, like as stews and dips.

6. **Num Banh Chok:** These are fresh rice noodles that are typically served with fresh veggies and a green curry sauce with a fish basis. It's a tasty and light dinner.

7. **Banh Chiao:** A crispy rice flour crepe stuffed with pork, shrimp, bean sprouts, and herbs, Banh Chiao is the Cambodian counterpart of the Vietnamese pancake. You dunk it in fish sauce and wrap it in lettuce.

8. **Fried Tarantulas (A-Ping):** Fried tarantulas are a special street cuisine from Cambodia that is recommended for the daring diner. They are frequently served with a hot dipping sauce and are crunchy.

9. Fresh tropical fruits abound in Sihanoukville, making fruit shakes and smoothies a popular beverage. Taste a

fruit shake or smoothie that contains dragon fruit, pineapple, coconut, mango, and other ingredients.

10. **Fresh Seafood**: Sihanoukville, a beach town, is well-known for its fresh seafood. Savour regionally inspired cuisine such as grilled fish, prawns, crab, and squid.

11. **Pizza Amok Fish:** This is a special fusion cuisine that mixes the flavours of traditional Cambodian amok with a crispy crust. It's a tasty and novel way to enjoy food.

12. Rice with Mango (Num Ansom): A sweet delicacy to cap off your dinner. Num Ansom is sticky rice with delicious, ripe mango slices inside, wrapped in banana leaves. It is a very tasty dessert.

13. Num Krok, a sweet potato dessert with coconut milk, is available at local markets. Num Krok is made out of sweet potato cakes and tiny, sweet, slightly crispy coconut milk cakes.

Sihanoukville offers a gateway to sample many of these classic delicacies from Cambodia's rich and varied culinary heritage. When you visit, don't miss the opportunity to sample the cuisine and discover Cambodia's unique flavours.

Popular Restaurants and Cafés

There are many cafés and restaurants in Sihanoukville that serve a range of cuisines, including international and Khmer delicacies.

The following well-known restaurants are worth checking out when you're there:

Eateries:

1. Fresh seafood and international cuisine are the main features of The Harbor Restaurant, a fine dining establishment situated within the Sokha Beach Resort. The restaurant's stunning waterfront location is ideal for a special evening meal for two.

2. **Sandan**: Known for its Khmer and Western fusion cuisine, Sandan is a member of the Friends International network. Not only is it a terrific location to eat, but it also helps underprivileged youngsters by offering vocational training.

3. **Holy Cow:** A well-known Indian eatery, Holy Cow offers a large selection of tantalising curries, tandoori meals, and vegetarian options. Both residents and visitors adore it.

4. **Fresh House**: Fresh seafood and Khmer cuisine are the specialties of this small restaurant. You can eat outside on the sand while taking in stunning views of the ocean.

5. French restaurant La Paillote is well-known for its delectable French and European fare. The steaks and seafood are excellent choices.

6. **Phsar Leu Restaurant:** This neighbourhood restaurant, which is situated in the centre of Phsar Leu Market, provides genuine Cambodian cuisine at incredibly low costs. Taste foods like fish amok and beef loc lac.

7. **Sunset Café:** This seaside eatery is well-known for its fresh seafood, drinks, and barbecue fare. It's a

well-liked location for dining and taking in the sunset.

Cafés:

1. **Koffie's Story:** A quaint café serving a selection of espresso and coffee drinks. It's a wonderful spot to unwind and sip coffee.

2. **The Daily Grind**: This café is a must-visit if you enjoy smoothies and fresh fruit shakes. In addition, they provide salads, sandwiches, and breakfast dishes.

3. **Rumi Café:** Rumi Café is well-known for its welcoming personnel, comfortable setting, and an assortment of Khmer and international cuisine. They provide a library for bookworms and serve a decent selection of beverages.

4. **Café Sushi:** This is a wonderful option if you're seeking Japanese food. They provide other popular Japanese dishes in addition to freshly made sushi and sashimi.

5. Home and Above Located on a rooftop terrace, this café provides an amazing view of the coastline of Sihanoukville. It's a lovely spot to eat and enjoy the surroundings while sipping coffee.

6. **4M Coffee**: Enjoy coffee brewed in Cambodia at this well-known neighbourhood café. They provide a variety of appetisers and coffee drinks.

Sihanoukville's restaurant and café scene offers a variety of dining options to suit a wide range of palates. You'll find plenty to sate your appetite, whether it's for world food, Khmer cuisine, or just a nice cup of coffee.

Street Food Adventures

Discovering Sihanoukville's street cuisine is a delectable journey that lets you enjoy real Cambodian cuisines and take in the local way of life. Try these suggestions for street food:

1. Find street sellers or little local restaurants that serve fish amok, a staple of Cambodia. Curry made with creamy coconut milk and usually served in banana leaves is called fish amok.

2. Nom Banh Chok is a well-liked morning meal in Cambodia. Fresh rice noodles with a variety of flavorful toppings and a green curry sauce made with fish are sold by street vendors.

3. **Seafood that has been grilled**: Sihanoukville's coastline location makes a plentiful supply of fresh seafood available. Sample the grilled fish, prawns, and squid that street sellers are selling. They frequently come with a delectable dipping sauce.

4. **Khmer BBQ**: Seek out street vendors selling barbecue. Meat and vegetable skewers marinated in sauce will be placed on your table for grilling. The dining experience is lively and engaging.

5. **Num Pang**: Num pang, a baguette sandwich with grilled meat, veggies, and sauces, is Cambodia's version of the banh mi. It is inspired by French cuisine. It's a convenient and filling street food choice.

6. **Fried Noodles:** Stir-fried noodles are frequently made by street vendors using a combination of veggies and protein. Using various sauces and spice levels, you can tailor the dish to your personal preferences.

7. Try fried tarantulas (A-Ping) if you're up for an adventurous meal. Sihanoukville street vendors often sell these crispy arachnids. The natives love this as a snack.

8. **Fruit Shakes and Smoothies**: Fresh fruit shakes and smoothies are sold by vendors in Sihanoukville, which is home to an abundance of tropical fruits. Experiment with pairings such as dragon fruit and passion fruit or mango and pineapple.

9. **Grilled corn**: Street vendors use open flames to roast corn on the cob and

provide a variety of sauces and seasonings to improve the flavour. It's an easy yet delicious snack.

10. **Kralan**: A well-liked snack in Cambodia, kralan is created with roasted red beans and sticky rice in bamboo tubes. Seek out merchants offering these mouthwatering sweets.

11. **Pong Aime**: Pong Aime is a well-known delicacy from Cambodia that is prepared by steaming glutinous rice, coconut cream, and palm sugar before it is wrapped in banana leaves.

When consuming street food in Sihanoukville, make sure to adhere to sanitary regulations by selecting vendors who have a high client turnover rate and spotless cooking spaces. Eating street food from the area is a terrific way to experience the local flavours and culture, and it's usually safe to consume. Asking locals or other travellers for tips on the best street food booths in the neighbourhood is a great idea.

Nightlife in Sihanoukville

Sihanoukville has a thriving nighttime culture with a wide range of entertainment options, including clubs and beachside bars. Here are a few of Sihanoukville's popular nightlife spots:

1. Serendipity Beach: Sihanoukville's nightlife is centred on Serendipity Beach. It is the preferred location for beach parties, live music, and dancing. It is surrounded by a large number of clubs and restaurants.

   There are beachside bars that feature fire shows, reggae music, and a lively vibe that carries over late into the evening.

2. **Otres Beach:** In contrast to Serendipity Beach, Otres Beach has a more laid-back nighttime atmosphere. There are beachside bars with comfy seats, great energy, and live music. It's a wonderful spot to sip a cocktail and take in the sunset.

3. Sihanoukville's downtown area offers a good selection of eateries, pubs, and nightclubs. This vibrant location is perfect for anyone looking to discover the city's nightlife since several venues feature live music and dancing.

4. **Casinos**: There are several casinos in Sihanoukville where you can test your luck at different games. Live entertainment and bars can be found in certain casinos.

5. **Nightclubs**: While beach bars and lounges are the mainstay of Sihanoukville's nightlife, there are a few nightclubs in the region where you can dance to the newest songs and take in DJ performances.

6. **Late-night Eateries**: After a night on the town, you can grab a bite to eat or a late-night snack at Sihanoukville's street food sellers and restaurants. Try some foreign or local Cambodian cuisine.

7. **Beach Parties**: A lot of seaside bars throw dances, bonfires, and DJs for their beach parties. These gatherings are particularly well-liked by tourists seeking an exciting and vibrant nightlife.

8. **Live Music:** Be on the lookout for locations that offer live music. In Sihanoukville, local and international musicians frequently perform, fostering a vibrant local music scene.

9. **Karaoke Bars:** In Cambodia, karaoke is a well-liked pastime. You can sing along with pals in karaoke bars.

10. **Pub crawls:** As you'll be visiting several pubs and getting to know other visitors, going on a pub crawl might be a great way to see Sihanoukville's nightlife.

11. **Boat Parties:** A few tour companies provide coast-cruising boat parties. These boat parties frequently have dancing, music, and a joyous vibe.

Please be aware that Sihanoukville's nightlife culture is subject to change, therefore it's a good idea to ask locals or other travellers for advice as venues' levels of popularity might fluctuate. In addition, have fun with the nightlife, but remember to drink sensibly and abide by local laws and customs.

ACTIVITIES AND ADVENTURES

Adventures and Activities in Cambodia's Sihanoukville

Situated on Cambodia's southwest coast, Sihanoukville is a coastal paradise offering a wide range of visitor activities and adventures.

Sihanoukville offers something for everyone, whether your preference is for exhilarating outdoor adventures or tranquil beaches for relaxation. We'll explore the best experiences and activities in this tropical paradise in this guide.

Water Activities:
1. Sihanoukville is a wonderful destination for anyone who enjoys the sea because of its coastline position,

which provides a variety of water sports and aquatic activities.

2. Snorkelling and diving: Novice and expert divers alike are drawn to the Gulf of Thailand's pristine waters. Discover a variety of aquatic life, including colourful fish and seahorses, by exploring vivid coral reefs.

   All skill levels can participate in PADI certification courses and diving excursions offered by Sihanoukville dive shops and travel operators.

3. **Jet-skiing and parasailing**: If you're looking for an exhilarating experience, you may hire jet skis and hit the waves, or you can parasail and soar over the water.

   These pursuits provide a view of Sihanoukville's stunning coastline from the perspective of an adrenaline seeker.

4. **Kayaking and paddleboarding**: Sihanoukville's tranquil waters are perfect for these water sports. You are free to take your time discovering remote beaches, mangroves, and secret coves.

5. **Fishing and Island Tours**: Take an island hopping tour or fishing excursion to explore neighbouring islands such as Koh Rong and Koh Rong Samloem. Fishing, snorkelling, and the opportunity to unwind on immaculate beaches are frequently included in these trips.

6. **Kitesurfing and windsurfing**: Otres Beach is a windsurfing and kitesurfing hotspot with steady winds. Those that

are interested can rent tools or enrol in classes at nearby schools.

7. **Boat Tours:** Take a leisurely boat cruise to discover the surrounding coastal regions and islands. Numerous cruises provide the chance to swim, sunbathe, and see dolphins in their native environment.

Visiting Islands:

1. The gateway to Cambodia's enchanted islands, each providing a distinctive experience, is Sihanoukville.

2. **Koh Rong:** A well-liked vacation spot, Koh Rong is well-known for its lively nightlife and white sand beaches.

   During the day, you may go on hikes through the jungle, visit waterfalls, and engage in water sports. At night, there are beach parties.

3. **Koh Rong Samloem**: Go to Koh Rong Samloem for a more sedate island experience. It's a perfect getaway with its calm beaches, glistening oceans, and starry nights. For a breathtaking experience, dive or snorkel with bioluminescent plankton.

4. **Koh Ta Kyiv:** If you're looking for an outdoor experience, Koh Ta Kyiv is the place to go. You may explore immaculate beaches, stroll through the woods, and even stay in beachside bungalows on this undeveloped, rustic island.

5. **Koh Thmei:** A beautiful and remote island experience, Koh Thmei is a part of Ream National Park. It's a nature lover's paradise with lots of

opportunities for mangrove exploration and birdwatching.

Nature tours and trekking:

There are many chances to explore the great outdoors and abundant natural beauty in Sihanoukville and the surrounding area.

1. Ream National Park is a nature lover's dream come true. You may go on guided hikes through verdant rainforests, see a variety of birds, and get up close and personal with reptiles and monkeys. There are also boat tours offered through the mangroves of the park.

2. **Trekking through the rainforests:** Explore the neighbouring rainforests, including the one on Koh Rong. You can explore the island's pristine interior, abundant flora, and secret

waterfalls by going on guided forest walks.

3. **Eco-Tourism**: Several Sihanoukville-based tour companies provide eco-tours that emphasise environmentally friendly and ethical travel. These trips frequently involve stops at nearby towns so guests can experience local culture firsthand.

4. **Bike Tours**: Rent a bike or sign up for a bike trip to discover Sihanoukville's rural and coastal regions. It's a great opportunity to take in the fresh sea wind and take in the sights at your speed.

Wellness and Yoga Retreats:

1. Sihanoukville, which offers yoga retreats and holistic experiences, has

become a popular destination for wellness and self-care.

2. **Yoga and meditation:** Yoga lessons and meditation sessions are offered by several resorts and wellness centres in Sihanoukville. These events are frequently hosted in calm coastal locations.

3. **Spa and Wellness Centers:** Indulge in wellness therapies, massages, and spa treatments that will help you feel refreshed. Numerous resorts provide holistic experiences that focus on well-being and relaxation.

4. **Retreats for Detox & Cleanse:** If you need a wellness makeover, think about taking part in one of these programs. These programs frequently include detoxification therapies, nutritious food, and yoga.

5. Retreats for Mindfulness and Healing: Sihanoukville offers the ideal setting for retreats centred around mindfulness and healing. Participate in programs that emphasise emotional health and self-discovery.

Sihanoukville is the perfect location for outdoor enthusiasts, beach lovers, wellness seekers, and nature aficionados because of the wide variety of activities and adventures available.

Sihanoukville has much to offer, whether you're searching for an exhilarating water sports experience, a tranquil island getaway, a hike through verdant jungles, or a wellness retreat by the sea.

It's a location where you may re-establish a connection with nature, revitalise your soul, and make lifelong memories that will be cherished long after you depart this idyllic coastal town.

DAY TRIPS FROM SIHANOUKVILLE

Koh Rong and Koh Rong Samloem

Off the coast of Sihanoukville, Cambodia, are two breathtaking islands that each provide a distinctive island experience: Koh Rong and Koh Rong Samloem. A closer look at these stunning locations is provided here:

Rong Koh:

1. **Bright Nightlife:** Koh Rong is well-known for having a vibrant nightlife. After dusk, the island comes alive with music events, fire shows, and beach parties. Globally renowned locations such as Police Beach and the Island Boys' gatherings attract revellers.

2. **Pristine Beaches:** There are several different, charming pristine beaches on the island. One of the best beaches is Long Beach (4K Beach), which has fine white sand and pristine waters. You can also visit Coconut Beach, Sok San Beach, and other locations.

3. **Water Sports:** For those who love the water, Koh Rong is a paradise. You can give kayaking, paddleboarding, diving, and snorkelling a try.

   The underwater environment of the island is rich and varied, with a wide variety of marine life and vibrant coral reefs.

4. **Jungle Adventures:** Koh Rong's interior is verdant and pristine. Discovering the natural splendour of the island can be greatly enhanced by trekking into the jungle. You can explore the

surrounding flora and fauna and find hidden waterfalls.

5. **Bioluminescent Plankton**: At night, Koh Rong's seas are illuminated by this unusual natural phenomenon. Swimming in the glistening, dazzling water is a once-in-a-lifetime adventure.

6. **Accommodations**: Koh Rong has a variety of lodging choices, ranging from boutique beachside resorts to affordable hostels. You can choose to rest in a more sedate location or stick close to the bustling party sections.

Samloem Koh Rong:

1. **Calm Haven**: Koh Rong Samloem, which is southwest of Koh Rong, offers a more sedate and calm environment. It's perfect for people looking for a

tranquil getaway from the busyness of everyday life.

2. **Crystal-Clear Waters**: The island is well-known for having immaculate beaches and crystal-clear waters. A well-liked location, Saracen Bay is noted for its expansive sandy beach and tranquil ambiance.

3. Diving and snorkelling are excellent in the waters surrounding Koh Rong Samloem.

   Discover the variety of aquatic life and the vibrant coral gardens. Compared to its more populated neighbour, the island has more isolated snorkelling locations.

4. **Eco-Friendly Accommodations**: Koh Rong Samloem offers a wide variety of lodging options that prioritise

sustainability and eco-friendliness. There are eco-resorts, beachside cabins, and quaint bungalows where you may unwind.

5. **Hiking and Nature trails**: There are hiking and nature trails available in the comparatively underdeveloped interior of the island. You can stroll through the verdant bush and find vantage points with magnificent views.

6. **Starry Nights**: Koh Rong Samloem is a great spot for stargazing because there isn't much artificial lighting on the island. You can gaze at the stars and constellations because the night skies are frequently clear.

Both islands provide a variety of lodging options, recreational opportunities, and scenic splendour and are reachable from Sihanoukville by boat. All travellers will have a memorable time on these islands, whether they are drawn to Koh Rong's lively party scene or Koh Rong Samloem's tranquil and immaculate beaches.

Kampot and Kep

Two quaint locations in southern Cambodia that are well-known for their natural beauty, extensive histories, and distinctive experiences are Kampot and Kep. A closer look at each of these charming towns is provided here:

Campo:

1. Beautiful Riverfront Town: Kampot is a charming riverfront town with a relaxed vibe.

   The village is traversed by the placid Praek Tuek Chhu River, which offers lovely vistas and riverfront dining options.

1. **Colonial Architecture**: There are several well-preserved buildings from the French colonial era in Kampot, a city rich in colonial architecture.

   You'll come across charming buildings and streets that transport you to another period as you stroll about the town.

2. **Pepper Plantations**: The Kampot region is well-known for producing some of the world's best pepper, which is of exceptional quality. To witness the cultivation and processing of this well-known spice, you can go to pepper plantations.

3. **Bokor National Park**: This neighbouring park has historical ruins, waterfalls, and beautiful jungles.

Discover the historic French hill station and take in the breathtaking views of the coast from the summit.

4. **Caving**: There are several caverns in the Kampot area, including the well-known Phnom Chhngok Cave Temple. These caves are significant culturally and have distinctive geological characteristics.

5. **Activities on the Water**: You may go kayaking, stand-up paddleboarding, or even enjoy riverboat rides. The serene canals encircling Kampot offer the ideal environment for these pursuits.

6. **Koh Tonsay (Rabbit Island):** Just a short boat journey from Kep, Rabbit Island is a serene tropical haven renowned for its immaculate beaches and laid-back atmosphere. Swimming, snorkelling, and dining on fresh

seafood at the island's restaurants are great ways to pass the time.

Kep

1. **Beach Charm:** Kep is a sleepy beach town well-known for its serene atmosphere and breathtaking scenery. For those who want to unwind and experience a slower pace of life, this is the perfect place to go.

2. **Crab Market:** Fresh seafood, particularly blue crab, is the specialty of the well-known Kep Crab Market. Among the many shacks and restaurants in the market, you may observe the local fisherman at work and enjoy mouthwatering seafood delicacies.

3. Kep National Park is an ideal destination for those who enjoy the

outdoors. Hiking through the park's verdant forests and exploring its pathways will lead you to viewpoints with expansive views of the surrounding ocean.

4. **Salt Fields:** The people of Kep are well-known for their salt fields, where they draw salt from the sea. To find out more about the process of producing salt and its importance to the neighbourhood, you can go on a guided tour.

5. **Kep Beach**: This area of the coast is calm and deserted. Though it's not a bathing beach, it's a great place for strolls, picnics, and soaking up the sea breeze.

6. Kep is home to a unique statue in the shape of a crab that has grown to be recognized as the town's landmark. The

statue is sometimes connected to Kep's well-known crab delicacies.

7. **Caves and Caverns**: There are a few caves and caverns in Kep that are worth exploring, such as the Phnom Kampong Trach and Phnom Sorsir caves.

   These caverns are cultural places with distinctive limestone formations.

Given their proximity, it is convenient to visit both Kampot and Kep when travelling in southern Cambodia. Every resort has a unique charm that draws in different kinds of tourists.

These charming villages have a lot to offer, whether your interests are in history, the outdoors, seafood, or just lounging by the sea.

Historical Sites

The regions surrounding Kampot and Kep in southern Cambodia are rich in historical and cultural significance. Here are a few historical locations in the area worth seeing:

Kampot District:

1. **Bokor Hill Station:** A French colonial hill station, Bokor Hill Station is situated inside Bokor National Park. It has a historic church and colonial structures that have been conserved.

   It's a wonderful historical and natural destination to visit because of the chilly climate and expansive views.

2. **Teuk Chhou Rapids**: An old bridge from the French colonial era once stood at these rapids, giving them historical significance. It's interesting to

investigate the bridge's ruins and the surrounding buildings.

3. The Kampot Provincial Museum provides information on the history and culture of the area. Photographs, relics, and historical details about Kampot are on exhibit.

Province of Kep:

1. **Kep Beach:** Although it's most recognized for its serene atmosphere, Kep Beach has a past. There are still traces of the elites' coastal villas from when Kep was a seaside getaway during the French colonial era.

2. **Crab Market:** Kep's Crab Market is a historical monument as well as a destination for fresh seafood. Kep's maritime past comes to life in the

market area with its quaint antique fishing shacks and boats.

3. **Kep National Park:** The park features historical components in addition to its natural attractions. Explore the remnants of a former French colonial-era casino, providing a window into Kep's opulent past as a posh resort community.

The island of Rabbit, Koh Tonsay:

1. Local Fishing Communities: You may visit Rabbit Island and have a tour of the local fishing communities there.

These villages provide a window into the customs of the nearby fishing villages.

The caves of Phnom Sorsia and Phnom Kampong Trach:

1. **Cultural Significance:** These caves are historically and culturally significant, and they are situated close to Kep. They have long been used for religious purposes and house shrines and Buddhist temples.

These historical buildings and landmarks provide a glimpse into southern Cambodia's past.

Discovering these locations will help you gain a greater understanding of the history of the area and how it contributed to the development of Cambodia, regardless of your interests in colonial history, cultural heritage, or the ruins of beachside resorts.

Off-the-beaten-path Excursions

Discovering off-the-beaten-path adventures in Kampot and Kep, Cambodia, can reveal undiscovered treasures and unforgettable experiences. The following are some lesser-known locations and things to think about:

Kampot District:

1. **Phnom Chhnork:** Compared to other cave sites, the Phnom Chhnork Cave Temple receives fewer visitors. There's a secret temple within that has old stalactites and stalagmites.

2. The Secret Lake, also known as Kampong Bay, is a remote location with a calm lake encircled by dense foliage. You can have a peaceful picnic by the lake's edge or rent a kayak or paddleboard to explore its tranquil waters.

3. **Cycling in the Countryside:** Grab a bike and head out into the gorgeous countryside that surrounds Kampot. You'll experience tranquil surroundings, quaint villages, and rural scenery.

4. **Climbing at Climbodia:** In a stunning natural setting, Climbodia provides rock climbing and bouldering experiences for those seeking adventure. For those who want to spice up their vacation with a little adventure, this is the ideal spot.

Province of Kep:

1. **Visits to Pepper Plantations:** Although many tourists go to Kampot, you can also discover the less well-known pepper farms in Kep. These farms

frequently provide quieter, more individualised tours.

2. **Kep Gardens**: Kep Gardens is a neighbourhood initiative that blends sustainability and agriculture. To see the lovely gardens and discover more about organic agricultural methods, you can take a guided tour.

3. **Koh Tonsay Beach Exploration**: There are more peaceful stretches of sand on Rabbit Island (Koh Tonsay) beyond the main beach. These are ideal for a peaceful picnic by the sea or a peaceful getaway.

4. **Sunset at Veranda Natural Resort**: Kep's Veranda Natural Resort boasts breathtaking views of the ocean at sunset. It's not necessary to be a guest to take in the sunset from their lovely

terrace. For those looking for a tranquil sunset experience, it's a hidden gem.

5. **Experiences on a Rural Island**: Koh Sdach and Koh Ses, two less-travelled islands close to Kep, provide an opportunity to see rural island villages and the real way of life in Cambodia. The developed areas are more developed than these islands.

6. **Adventures in Marine Conservation**: Several Kep-based organisations are dedicated to marine conservation.

   Take into consideration signing up for a tour or volunteer program that will let you learn about coastal habitats and help with conservation efforts.

Discovering these off-the-beaten-path adventures can bring you a more personal and distinctive look into the Kampot and Kep area. It enables you to experience a more laid-back and uncrowded atmosphere, uncover hidden natural treasures, and establish a connection with the local culture.

PRACTICAL INFORMATION

Money and Currency

The Cambodian Riel (KHR) is the official currency of Cambodia, although US dollars (USD) are also commonly accepted and utilised in day-to-day transactions. The following are important details regarding money and currencies in Cambodia:

1. The official currency of Cambodia is the Cambodian Riel (KHR), yet most small-scale transactions use it. The denominations of banknotes are 50, 100, 500, 1000, 2000, 5000, 10,000, 20,000, 50,000, and 100,000 Riel, among others. The Cambodian Riel's currency code is KHR.

2. **United States Dollar (USD)**: The USD is the main form of currency used for major purchases, including

reservations for hotels, tours, and dining out, and it is widely recognized in Cambodia. You can pay in either currency, and many prices are quoted in both Riel and USD. For convenience, it's a good idea to keep some USD on hand in small denominations.

3. **Currency Exchange:** In large towns like Phnom Penh and Siem Reap, banks and money exchange counters are where you may exchange your foreign currency, including USD and major international currencies.

   Even if you pay in USD, you could still receive a change in Cambodian Riel.

4. **ATMs**: Most metropolitan ATMs accept major international credit and debit cards, and they are generally accessible. ATMs allow you to take out both USD and Riel, albeit USD is the

more popular option. Recognize that certain ATMs could impose a fee for withdrawals.

5. **Credit and Debit Cards:** Upmarket hotels, restaurants, and shops accept major credit and debit cards, including Visa and MasterCard. However, in many locations, particularly in more rural areas, cash is still the preferred form of payment.

6. Traveler's checks are not often accepted in Cambodia, and it could be difficult to locate establishments that do. Using cash, credit/debit cards, or local money is advised.

7. **Currency Exchange Rates:** Before exchanging your money, it is essential to confirm the current exchange rates, as they are subject to change. A lot of

banks and exchange offices publicly post their rates.

8. **Currency Advice:** Make sure your bills are in good condition when handling currency because they can be rejected if they are torn or damaged.

   When getting change, use caution because counterfeit money can be dangerous, particularly in lower denominations.

9. **Tipping**: Although not required, tipping is valued in Cambodia. 10% is the standard gratuity for services and restaurants. Make sure your gratuity is presented to the servers immediately; if you leave it on the table, it might not get to them.

When visiting Cambodia, it is advisable to have a combination of US dollars and

Cambodian Riel with you, as this will facilitate the payment of different bills. Even though USD is frequently recognized, minor purchases and transactions in more rural or localised regions may benefit from having some Riel on hand.

Communication

English is widely spoken in metropolitan areas of Cambodia, especially by individuals working in the tourism sector, and communication is often easy. Here are a few essential details regarding communication in Cambodia:

1. **Language**: The majority of people in Cambodia speak Khmer, which is the official language of the country.

   Even though not everyone speaks English well, many people in major towns and tourist destinations like

Phnom Penh, Siem Reap, Sihanoukville, Kampot, and Kep can communicate in the language, particularly at hotels, restaurants, and other establishments that serve visitors.

2. **Salutations**: "Chum reap suor" (Hello) and "Sua s'dei" (How are you?) are typical greetings in Khmer. Utilising these salutations when speaking with natives is considerate.

   To a question like "How are you?" a straightforward "Sok sabay" (Good) is suitable. A small bow may be used to greet someone in a more formal environment.

3. **Gaining Knowledge of Basic Khmer**: Being able to communicate with locals can be greatly facilitated by learning a few simple Khmer phrases. Expressions such as "Som arkoun" (I'm grateful),

"Sampeah" (a traditional bow-based greeting from Cambodia), and "Lia suhn hao-y?" (What is the price of this?) may be useful.

4. **Local Etiquette**: Courtesies and dignity are highly prized in Cambodia. It is usual to take off your shoes when you go inside a place of worship or someone's house.

   Wear modest clothing, covering your knees and shoulders, when you visit temples. Minimal public expressions of affection are advised.

5. **Nonverbal Communication**: To express agreement or courtesy, Cambodians employ nonverbal clues like smiles and nods. It is considered impolite to point your feet at someone, especially a monk or a Buddha statue.

6. **Haggling**: Bargaining is a popular practice when purchasing at markets. Maintain a nice demeanour and negotiate rates in a firm but polite manner.

7. **Internet and Connectivity**: Free Wi-Fi is available in many locations, and Cambodia boasts a strong mobile network. To use data services, you can buy local SIM cards, which are reasonably priced and generally accessible.

8. **Emergency Services**: To contact the police in an emergency, phone 119, and to request medical aid, dial 117.

9. **Time Zone**: Cambodia is located seven hours ahead of Coordinated Universal Time (UTC+7) in the Indochina Time Zone (ICT).

10. **Electricity**: Type A and Type C electrical outlets are used in Cambodia. 50 Hz is the standard frequency, and 230 V is the standard voltage. Keeping a universal adaptor on hand for your electronics is advised.

11. **Postal Services**: Compared to certain other nations, Cambodia's postal system might not be as dependable. Check with your local post office or look into foreign courier services if you need to ship mail or packages.

Recall that most Cambodians are kind and open to visitors, so trying to pick up a few phrases in the local tongue and customs will improve your trip and encourage goodwill among the populace.

Safety Tips

Like any other place, travelling to Cambodia involves taking certain safety precautions and being aware of potential threats. The following safety advice should be kept in mind while you visit Cambodia:

1. **Health-Guard Measures:**

- Make sure all of your regular immunizations are current. Think about getting vaccinated against tetanus, typhoid, and hepatitis A.

- Seek guidance from a medical professional regarding immunizations and treatments for illnesses such as dengue and malaria, particularly if you want to travel to isolated regions.

- Use bottled water to brush your teeth and drink it. Steer clear of tap water and ice that has been prepared with it.

2. **Food Security:**

- Savour the gastronomy of Cambodia, but use caution while consuming street food from unclean stands. Choose vendors who have a high client turnover rate and spotless cooking spaces.

- Before consuming fruits and vegetables, peel or wash them.

3. **Insurance for Travel:**
- Invest in comprehensive travel insurance that includes coverage for lost or stolen personal belongings, medical emergencies, and trip cancellations.

4. **Money and Precious Items:**
- Only bring as much cash as you'll need for the day. To keep your valuables

safe, use lockable money belts or hotel safes.

- Use caution when utilising ATMs, particularly in remote or poorly lit locations. When entering your PIN, keep it covered.

5. **Transportation and Traffic:**

- When crossing roadways in a city, use caution. Pedestrians do not always have the right-of-way in busy traffic.

- Make sure you are wearing a helmet and that you have the required licences before hiring a scooter or motorcycle. Requirements for road safety may be less strict than in certain other nations.

6. **Deployed mines and detonated ordinance:**
- Despite advancements in demining, unexploded ordnance remains in some

places of Cambodia, particularly in the vicinity of the borders with Thailand and Laos. Avoid going into isolated, undeveloped areas without a local guide, and stick to designated routes.

7. Cultural Equality:

- Be mindful of others when you visit places of worship, including temples. Cover your legs and shoulders when you dress modestly. When you enter temple structures, take off your shoes.

- Monks should not be touched; in particular, ladies should not come into personal contact with them.

8. Bite From Insects and Preventing Disease:

- Avoid getting bitten by mosquitoes because there are parts of Cambodia where dengue and malaria are common. Wear long sleeves and pants and apply bug repellent, especially around nightfall and dawn.

9. Documentation for Travel:

- Copies of your visa, passport, and other critical documents should be kept apart from the originals. Maintaining safe digital copies is also a smart idea.

10. Regional scams

- Avoid falling for popular travel scams, such as being taken to businesses for commission or being overcharged by tuk-tuk drivers.

  Before boarding a tuk-tuk, agree on a price.

11. Emergency Number to Contact:

- Keep your phone loaded with the local emergency numbers, such as 119 for the police and 117 for medical aid.

12. Kids on the streets and begging:

- Regretfully, there are a lot of street children begging in Cambodia.

  Even though it's challenging, don't give them money as this will only make the problem worse. Instead, give your support to ethical organisations.

13. Travels & Outings:

- Select trustworthy and authorised tour and excursion providers when making your reservations. Get advice from other travellers by reading reviews.

14. **Political Signs and Protests**:

- Political protests should not be attended or observed, as they occasionally turn chaotic.

Although travel to Cambodia is typically secure, a smooth and pleasurable journey can be ensured by being aware of the local laws and customs, exercising common sense, and remaining informed.

It's also a good idea to see whether there are any special safety precautions for travelling to Cambodia listed in your nation's travel advice.

Health and Medical Services

It's crucial to look after your health and well-being while visiting Cambodia. The following are important things to remember about Cambodian health and medical services:

1. **Immunizations and Health Safety Measures:**

   - Make sure you have had all recommended immunizations before your travel by speaking with your healthcare provider.

   - Think about getting vaccinated against tetanus, typhoid, and hepatitis A.

   - It is advisable to consult your healthcare professional about the necessity of vaccinations or medications against diseases such as Japanese encephalitis, dengue, and malaria, particularly if you want to travel to isolated or rural regions.

2. **Healthcare Institutions:**

- English-speaking medical professionals can be found in contemporary clinics and hospitals in big cities like Phnom Penh and Siem Reap.

  There might not be as many medical facilities in remote locations, though.

- Calmette Hospital, Royal Phnom Penh Hospital, and SOS International Clinic are a few of the city of Phnom Penh's well-known medical facilities.

  One respectable choice in Siem Reap is the Royal Angkor International Hospital.

3. Insurance for Travel:

- Getting comprehensive travel insurance that covers medical emergencies, evacuation, and repatriation is strongly advised. Make sure your insurance covers the things you want to do in Cambodia.

4. Prescriptions & Medication:

- Bring a copy of the prescription and any relevant prescription drugs with you.

  Make sure you have enough medicine for the duration of your vacation.

- Local pharmacies may have certain over-the-counter medications, but it's advisable to pack necessities like pain relievers and any personal medications you frequently take.

5. Safety of Food and Water:

- Make thoughtful food and drink selections to avoid contracting foodborne illnesses. Remain with hot, prepared dishes and clean, peeled or sliced fruits and vegetables.

- Use the water from the bottle to brush your teeth and drink it. Steer clear of tap water and tap water-made ice.

6. Diseases Spread by Insects:

- There are regions in Cambodia where dengue fever and malaria are common.

  Use insect repellent, put on long sleeves and pants, and use bed nets if needed to protect yourself from mosquito bites.

7. Sun Shielding:

- Because of its tropical environment, sunburn could be an issue in Cambodia. Wear a wide-brimmed hat, use sunscreen with a high SPF, and drink plenty of water.

8. Diarrhoea from Travel:

- There may be a chance of traveller's diarrhoea in Cambodia. Keep over-the-counter drugs like loperamide on hand in case you need symptomatic relief. It's critical to maintain adequate hydration if you have diarrhoea.

9. Health Safety Measures:

- Swimming in freshwater bodies should be done with caution because some may have parasites that might infect you.

- When handling and eating street food, exercise caution. Choose providers who have spotless kitchens.

10. **Local Drugstores:**

- There are lots of pharmacies in Cambodia where you may get over-the-counter drugs and personal hygiene products. Still, it's a good idea to pack the necessary drugs.

11. **Emergencies**: -

- If you have a medical emergency, get in touch with the embassy or consulate of your nation, and they can help you find a hospital. In Cambodia, 117 is the local emergency number for medical assistance.

During your journey to Cambodia, it's critical to keep up with health and safety precautions, observe local customs, and practise proper hygiene. You may make sure that your trip is fun and free of serious health issues by being organised and cautious.

APPENDIX

Essential Useful Phrases

Understanding a few keywords in Khmer will improve your trip and enable you to interact with locals when you visit Sihanoukville and Cambodia. Here are a few helpful Khmer phrases:

- Hello: "Chum reap suor" (ជំរាបសួរ)
- How are you?: "Sua s'dei" (សួស្តី)
- Good: "Sok sabay" (សុខសបាយ)
- Thank you: "Som arkoun" (សូមអរគុណ)
- Yes: "Baht" (បាទ)
- No: "Ot" (អុត)
- Please: "Som" (សូម)
- Excuse me / Sorry: "Som thngai" (សូមថ្ងៃ)
- How much is this?: "Lia suhn hao-y?" (លិចសួនហេរ?)
- Where is...?: "Te na...?" (តែណា...?)

- I don't understand: "Knyom ot jol neak" (ខ្ញុំអុតចេត)
- Help: "Chomreang, som toht" (ជំរាបសំមេង, សូមតែព្រម)

Recall that pronouncing words in Khmer can differ from pronouncing them in English, so it's a good idea to practise.

Even if you can just speak a few simple words in their language, the locals will still appreciate your attempt. It can improve the way you interact with each other and add enjoyment to your trip.

Emergency Contacts and Information

Here are some crucial numbers and details you should be aware of in case of an emergency when visiting Sihanoukville, Cambodia:

Security Services:

- Police: To contact the police, dial 119.
- For emergency medical assistance, dial 117.

Consulates and Embassies:

- Having the contact details for your nation's embassy or consulate in Cambodia is a wise move.

  In the event of an emergency, they can help with missing passports, legal matters, or medical crises.

Medical Establishments:

- If you have more significant medical problems, you might choose to visit one of the respected hospitals in Sihanoukville or one of the larger neighbouring towns, such as Phnom Penh or Siem Reap.

  Calmette Hospital, Royal Phnom Penh Hospital, SOS International Clinic, and the Royal Angkor International Hospital in Siem Reap are a few of the well-known hospitals.

nearby pharmacies

- Both Sihanoukville and other urban regions have a large number of pharmacies. These pharmacies sell both typical prescription drugs and personal hygiene products.

Insurance for Travel:

- Make sure your travel insurance is comprehensive and covers repatriation, evacuation, and medical situations. Carry a duplicate of your insurance policy and contact information in case of emergency.

Neighborhood Police Posts:

- Find out the address and phone number of the police station closest to your lodging. They can help with small problems and mishaps.

Passport misplaced or stolen:

- To report a lost or stolen passport, get in touch with the local police. After that, ask your embassy or consulate for advice on how to obtain a substitute.

Having these figures and details on hand can help you feel more at ease when travelling. When travelling in Cambodia, never forget to prioritise your safety and well-being, travel with caution, and abide by local laws.